LEARNING ABOUT
PRAYER

Lois Rock

Illustrated by Maureen Galvani

WARNER *Faith*

Acknowledgment: Scripture taken from the *Good News Bible* in Today's English Version, Second Edition, copyright © 1992 by American Bible Society. Used by permission.

Text copyright © 2003 by Lion Publishing
Illustrations copyright © 2003 by Maureen Galvani

First U.S. Edition
First published in Great Britain by Lion Publishing in 2002

ISBN 0-446-53297-5
LCCN 2002117761

10 9 8 7 6 5 4 3 2 1

Printed in Singapore

The text was set in Apollo MT, and the display type is Kidprint MT.

Introduction: What is prayer?

 Prayer means spending time with God.

When you spend time with a friend, you often talk. You also listen. Sometimes you just sit quietly together.

We believe that praying to God is like that — it is like being with a very special kind of friend. This book will tell you more about what we mean by prayer.

1. Who is a prayer said to?

When we pray, we pray to God.

Sometimes we begin as if we are speaking to a grand person: "O God."

Sometimes we begin in the same way that people begin a letter: "Dear God."

Sometimes we use a title — words that say something about who God is: "O Lord" or "Heavenly Father." There are many more titles.

Sometimes we begin with whatever we really want to say, and we believe that God will hear us.

 We speak to God in prayer with respect and trust.

2. Do people have to say prayers really loud for God to hear?

We believe that God cannot be seen but is everywhere and knows everything.

We believe God can hear a prayer even when we think it instead of saying it.

Sometimes we say our prayers aloud, but quietly, even if we are alone.

When we meet with other Christians, we often say prayers quite loudly so they can all hear and think the prayer, too, if they want.

We believe that God hears every kind of prayer, loud or silent.

3. Does a prayer have to have special words?

We believe that God understands a person's prayer, no matter which words they choose.

Jesus, the one whom we follow, gave his followers a short and simple prayer to use:

Father:

May your holy name be honored;

may your Kingdom come.

Give us day by day the food we need.

Forgive us our sins,

for we forgive everyone who does us wrong.

And do not bring us to hard testing.

We pray to God with simple words, such as the ones Jesus taught.

4. Do people have to learn prayers or can they make them up?

We believe that prayer is what people say to God from the heart.

Our own prayers are very important to God, even if the words don't seem very clever.

We also use prayers that we learn in other ways: prayers that we find in the Bible and prayers written by other Christians.

Sometimes, we ask other Christians to pray for us.

Whatever the words, we believe that real prayer is from the heart.

5. Isn't there a magic word that makes a prayer real?

Many Christians end their prayers with a special word: "Amen."

It simply means "let it be so."

It isn't magic, and it doesn't have to be said at all, but all over the world it is a traditional way of marking the end of a prayer.

When we pray together, one person may say the prayers aloud, and we will all join in the "Amen" to show that we are joining in the whole prayer.

We believe that prayer is real because God is listening.

6. Aren't some prayers to Jesus?

We believe that Jesus is God's Son.

We believe that Jesus also hears our prayers, and we often pray to Jesus. Sometimes it seems easier to pray to the God-who-is-Jesus because Jesus was a human being just like us. It is easy to picture what he is like and to imagine talking to him.

Our prayers may begin like this: "Dear Jesus," "Lord Jesus," or "Christ Jesus." "Christ" is a title meaning "God's chosen king."

Sometimes we pray to God but end our prayers with the words "in Jesus' name."

 We believe that Jesus hears our prayers.

7. Do people have to sit in a special way to pray?

There are several different traditions for how people pray.

Some Christians kneel to pray.

Some stand up.

Some hold their palms up.

Some put their hands together.

Some look up while others look down, and still others close their eyes.

Whatever the tradition we usually follow, we believe that God will always hear us whenever we pray.

We believe that God hears our prayers no matter how we are praying.

8. Do people have to go to a special place to pray?

We like to meet to learn about God and to worship God.
Our gathering place is called a church.

We will pray wherever we gather: sometimes in a room in a house, sometimes in a church building.

Jesus also told his followers to make their own prayer a quiet and private thing.
He said that we can go into a room and close the door.

He himself sometimes went off for a walk to pray on his own in the countryside.

We think prayer is not something to show off about — it is between us and God.

We believe that we can pray in any place where, in our hearts, we are alone with God.

9. Is there a special time to pray?

We believe that God cares for the world day and night.
We believe we can pray to God at any time.

Sometimes we set aside a special time to pray, either alone
or together.

Sometimes we say a prayer as the
day begins…

before we eat a meal…

before we begin a journey…

and so on.

One tradition is to say a prayer asking for God's blessing before we go to sleep.

Here is a blessing from the Bible that is often said as a nighttime prayer:

"May the Lord bless you and take care of you."

 We believe that God hears our prayers at any time of day or night.

10. If you ask God for things, do you get them?

We believe that God wants people to enjoy life and all the good things it can bring.

We also believe that what makes people really happy is not things, but to be a close friend to God.

As we pray, God helps us to see what is important to happiness and what is not.

We believe that God wants to give people good things — and that he knows what is best for us.

11. If you pray for something bad, will it happen?

We believe that God is all good, and that God will never make anything bad happen.

Sometimes people who pray to God are very angry and they ask for bad things.

We believe that God will listen to them with great kindness. We also believe that God will help them find a good way out of being angry, and a good way to deal with the problem.

 We believe that prayer can only do good things, because God is good.

12. If God knows everything, why do people need to pray at all?

We believe that God already knows what people think and believe and need and want.

We also believe that people were made to be friends with God. Spending time in prayer helps to build that friendship.

As we pray, we begin to see things the way God sees them.

That changes everything!

We have begun a great friendship that we believe in our hearts will last forever and ever.

 We believe that prayer helps us to be friends with God forever.

What is prayer?

1. We speak to God in prayer with respect and trust.

2. We believe that God hears every kind of prayer, loud or silent.

3. We pray to God with simple words, such as the ones Jesus taught.

4. Whatever the words, we believe that real prayer is from the heart.

5. We believe that prayer is real because God is listening.

6. We believe that Jesus hears our prayers.

7. We believe that God hears our prayers no matter how we are praying.

8. We believe that we can pray in any place where, in our hearts, we are alone with God.

9. We believe that God hears our prayers at any time of day or night.

10. We believe that God wants to give people good things — and that he knows what is best for us.

11. We believe that prayer can only do good things, because God is good.

12. We believe that prayer helps us to be friends with God forever.